Truth and Rumors
Titanic

by Michael Burgan   illustrations by Eldon Doty

Consultant:
John P. Eaton, Historian
Titanic International Society
Freehold, New Jersey

CAPSTONE PRESS
a capstone imprint

Edge Books are published by Capstone Press,
151 Good Counsel Drive, P.O. Box 669, Mankato, Minnesota 56002.
www.capstonepress.com

Library of Congress Cataloging-in-Publication Data
Burgan, Michael.
    Titanic : truth and rumors / by Michael Burgan ; illustrated by Eldon Doty.
    p. cm. — (Edge books. Truth and rumors)
    Summary: "Labels common stories about the Titanic as fact or fiction and teaches readers
how to tell the difference between truth and rumors" — Provided by publisher.
    Includes bibliographical references and index.
    ISBN 978-1-4296-3951-4 (library binding)
    1. Titanic (Steamship) — Juvenile literature. 2. Shipwrecks — North Atlantic Ocean —
Juvenile literature. I. Doty, Eldon, ill. II. Title. III. Series.
G530.T6B853 2010
910.9163'4 — dc22   2009028656

Editorial Credits
Abby Czeskleba, editor; Tracy Davies; designer; Wanda Winch, media researcher;
    Nathan Gassman, art director; Laura Manthe, production specialist; Eldon Doty, illustrator

Photo Credits
AP Images: PA Files cover (Titanic); Art Life Images: age fotostock/Wojtek Buss 27;
The Bridgeman Art Library International: The Illustrated London News Picture Library,
London, UK/The famous iceberg as seen by J. Scarrott on board the Titanic, 1912 14 (bottom);
Corbis: Bettmann 20 (bottom), Christie's Images 7, Hulton-Deutsch Collection 5; iStockphoto:
Bill Noll cover (brown texture); Library of Congress: cover (Molly Brown), 10 (bottom), 19; Mary
Evans Picture Library: 12 (both), 18 (bottom), 22 (top); National Museums Northern Ireland,
Ulster Folk and Transport Museum: (40253) 23, (Courtney #4) 9, (H1637) 17 (top), (H1732)
8 (bottom), (H2423) 11 (bottom); Newscom: Zuma live 26; Painting by Ken Marschall ©1992
15; RMS Titanic Inc: ©Bill Sauder Collection, www.rmstitanic.net 25 (bottom); Shutterstock:
Adam Radosavljevic cover, back cover (frames), Albachiara (quill pen/inkwell, throughout),
Ali Mazraie Shadi (halftone, throughout), Myszka Brudnicka cover, back cover (wallpaper),
Phase4Photography cover, back cover (floor), VikaSuh (gavel, throughout)

Table of Contents

Getting the Facts Right..4
Did *Titanic*'s owners claim
    the ship was unsinkable?.............................. 6
Was *Titanic* in a rush? 8
Was someone trapped inside *Titanic*'s hull? 10
Was the *Titanic* disaster
    predicted before 1912? 12
Did a long tear in the hull sink *Titanic*? 14
Were *Titanic* and *Olympic* switched?.............. 16
Did some of the lifeboats
    sail before they were full? 18
Did male passengers dress as women? 20
Did an officer kill a passenger? 22
Was there a fire on board *Titanic*? 24
Did the Hope diamond sink *Titanic*?...............26
Did a mummy's curse doom *Titanic*? 27
Fact or Fiction?: How to Tell the Difference.....28

Glossary 30
Read More 31
Internet Sites 31
Index 32

Getting the Facts Right

On April 15, 1912, more than 1,500 people died when *Titanic* sank. Ever since that day, the ship's deadly **maiden voyage** has fascinated people. But not all of the stories about the famous ship are true.

Facts and rumors can blend together to make for some interesting stories. If you dig deeper, you'll find out what really happened to *Titanic* and its passengers. Put on your detective hat and learn to sort the truth from the rumors.

maiden voyage – a ship's first trip

Did *Titanic's* owners claim the ship was unsinkable?

What's the story?

White Star officials said the ship could never sink. That's quite the claim for a ship that weighed more than 50,000 tons (45,359 metric tons) when fully loaded. But White Star officials were confident because *Titanic* had watertight **compartments** and other safety features. The compartments were supposed to keep the ship from flooding after an accident.

NOT SO FAST . . .

After the sinking, the ship's builders and owners said they never claimed *Titanic* couldn't sink. Some news reports published before *Titanic's* voyage said the ship was "practically unsinkable." People thought this meant that White Star officials believed the ship couldn't sink.

Maybe. A 1910 White Star advertisement for *Titanic* said the ship was "designed to be unsinkable." But later ads didn't make this claim. The day of the disaster, a White Star official told reporters, "We believe that the boat is unsinkable." The idea that an "unsinkable" ship didn't live up to its name fueled the interest in *Titanic*'s story.

compartment – a section inside a ship that is divided by walls and doors

Troubled "Sisters"

Titanic was one of three sister ships that looked almost completely alike. The ships all had problems at sea. *Olympic* ran into a tugboat on a trip to New York in 1911. *Olympic* suffered very little damage. But a few months later, the ship struck another ship in Southampton, England. This time, *Olympic* was badly damaged. The third sister ship was *Britannic*. During World War I (1914–1918), the British used it as a hospital ship. While cruising in the Aegean Sea, *Britannic* was hit by a mine. The ship sank in less than one hour.

Was *Titanic* in a rush?

What's the story?

After picking up the last passengers, *Titanic* raced across the Atlantic Ocean from Queenstown, Ireland, to New York. The ship's owners wanted *Titanic* to set a new speed record.

BUT CONSIDER THIS . . .

Titanic was the largest ship of its day. While it had elegant rooms and fine art unlike any other ship, it was not built for speed. It traveled about 5 **knots** slower than *Mauretania*, the fastest ship of the day.

No. *Titanic* was not trying to set a speed record. The ship was designed to be roomy and luxurious, not fast. People knew *Titanic* could never win the Blue Riband, the honor given to the fastest ship to cross the Atlantic Ocean.

knot – a measurement of speed for ships; 1 knot equals 1.15 miles (1.85 kilometers) per hour.

FACT: The most expensive rooms on *Titanic* cost more than $4,000 for the maiden voyage. Today, those rooms would cost almost $100,000 each.

Was someone trapped inside *Titanic*'s hull?

What's the story?

While the ship was being built, workers heard tapping from inside the ship's hull. In the rush to complete the ship, some workers were trapped inside the hull. The tapping noises were a call for help from the trapped workers.

WAIT A SECOND . . .

Workers built *Titanic* in Belfast, Ireland, from 1909 to 1911. During that time, inspectors often went inside the ship's hull. They rapped on it with hammers to test the work of the shipbuilders. Some men heard the tapping and may have thought workers were trapped inside.

Construction of *Titanic*'s hull in 1911

The VERDICT

COME ON, MEN... FASTER, FASTER!

No. Some workers thought they were being forced to build the ship too quickly. The shipbuilder was determined to finish *Titanic* on time. The workers may have started the rumor to make the company look bad. Some workers may have jokingly told new men on the job that the noise came from trapped workers.

FACT: The hull of *Titanic* was made out of large steel plates. Some plates were 30 feet (9 meters) long and 6 feet (1.8 meters) wide.

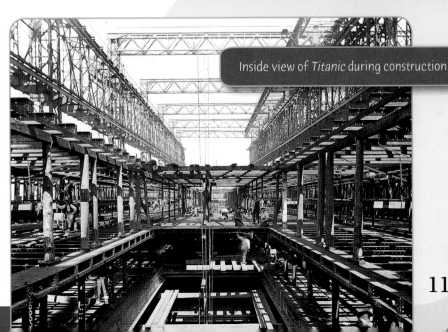

Inside view of *Titanic* during construction

Was the *Titanic* disaster predicted before 1912?

What's the story?

In 1898, Morgan Robertson published a short novel called *Futility*. It told of the sinking of a huge ocean liner on its maiden voyage. Robertson called the ship *Titan*.

WAIT A SECOND ...

According to Robertson's book, *Titan* was unsinkable and also the largest ship of its day. The ship sank after hitting an iceberg around midnight on an April evening. Robertson wrote many tales about life at sea. He knew about ship technology and what new developments were possible. *Futility* does share some amazing **coincidences** with *Titanic's* story.

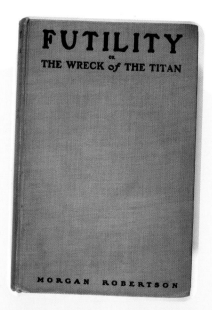

FUTILITY
OR.
THE WRECK of THE TITAN

MORGAN ROBERTSON

But *Titanic* was not the first ship to hit an iceberg. Hundreds of ships crashed into icebergs in the years before *Titanic* sailed. At least three ships called *Titania* sank before Robertson wrote his book. One of them also hit an iceberg. Robertson may have based his story on the past and not the future.

coincidence – a chance happening or meeting

FACT: Much like Morgan Robertson, *Titanic* passenger W. T. Stead wrote a book about the sinking of a great ship. Stead wrote his book in 1893. He died when *Titanic* sank, but he didn't seem scared when he boarded the ship.

The VERDICT

No. Most experts believe the stories of *Titan* and *Titanic* are just coincidences. Some scientists study claims about people who say they can predict the future. These scientists don't believe Robertson knew *Titanic* would sink years after he wrote the book.

Did a long tear in the hull sink *Titanic*?

What's the story?

The iceberg tore a 300-foot (91-meter) gash in the right side of the ship's hull. The gaping hole let water flow into large sections of the ship.

300 Feet!

BUT CONSIDER THIS . . .

BOAT DECK

DARK EARTHY PATCH

STARBOARD LIGHT

STARBOARD SHELTER ON BRIDG

PROMENADE DECK

LOOSE ICE

ICE ON WELL DECK

14

Shortly after *Titanic* sank, some experts began to question the **theory** about the long gash. But if there was no gash, how did the ship sink? One expert said *Titanic* could've hit pieces of ice that made many small holes. Years later, some scientists said the ship's bottom may have scraped along the iceberg. The hole on the ship's bottom might have caused the most damage.

No. Underwater research done in 1997 showed there was no long gash. Several small slits in the hull let in the water. Later studies of the wreck also proved there wasn't a hole on the ship's bottom.

theory – an idea that explains something that is unknown

Were *Titanic* and *Olympic* switched?

What's the story?

In 1995, journalists Robin Gardiner and Dan Van Der Vat wrote a book that made an amazing claim. When *Titanic*'s sister ship *Olympic* was damaged in 1911, White Star took the insurance money rather than use it for major repairs. White Star workers replaced everything that said *Olympic* with *Titanic*. The real *Titanic* later went to sea as *Olympic*.

WAIT A SECOND . . .

A theory like this one would've involved many people at White Star and the shipyard. They would've all had to agree to keep the secret forever. Gardiner and Van Der Vat may not have had much proof to support their theory. But they tried to show that White Star officials had a good reason to switch the ships.

No. Experts knew the ships weren't completely the same. Crew members of both ships noted differences between them. *Titanic* had a glassed-in deck, *Olympic* did not. Plus, each ship had a number stamped in many places, such as the hull. In recent years, divers have explored the shipwreck. *Titanic*'s number, 401, appears on the parts where the ship number would have been stamped.

Olympic (left) and *Titanic* (right) were sister ships.

Fake Photos — EXPOSED!

Think every picture you see of *Titanic* is really of the doomed ship? Many newspapers of the day used photos of *Olympic* in articles about *Titanic*. More photos of *Olympic* were available because the ship first sailed one year before *Titanic*. The two sister ships looked enough alike that few people ever knew they were actually seeing photos of *Olympic*.

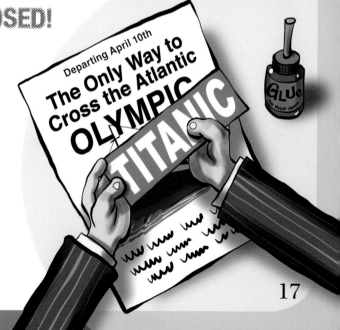

17

Did some of the lifeboats sail before they were full?

What's the story?

Titanic officers ordered some of the ship's 20 lifeboats to sail before they were filled with passengers.

OK, that's enough! Lower away!

BUT CONSIDER THIS . . .

Titanic carried more lifeboats than the law required. The 20 lifeboats could hold 1,178 people. After the sinking, two officers said they didn't go back to rescue drowning people. They were afraid the people would tip over the lifeboats.

Yes. At least six lifeboats were less than half full when they sailed. The crew allowed women and children to board the lifeboats first. But some women didn't rush to board the lifeboats when the ship started sinking. They thought there was no immediate danger and wanted to stay with their families. As *Titanic* sank, the officers could've let more men into the boats. The officers could've also waited until more passengers came to the boat stations. Another 500 people might have been saved if the boats hadn't been lowered so quickly. There were more than 2,200 people on the ship. Sadly, not everyone would've been saved even if the boats had been completely filled.

A Hero at Sea

U.S. millionaire Margaret "Molly" Brown became one of the heroes of the *Titanic* disaster. As the ship sank, Brown helped other women into the lifeboats. Once at sea, she challenged the man commanding the boat. He didn't want the women on board to row, but Brown insisted the women be allowed to help. She earned the nickname "Unsinkable Molly Brown." A movie musical of the same name was later made about her life.

Did male passengers dress as women?

What's the story?

Male passengers knew that women and children were first to board the lifeboats. Some men disguised themselves as women to make it on the lifeboats.

THE EVIDENCE

Men waited with women and children to board the lifeboats. Some officers let men board the boats. One woman gave a freezing sailor her shawl. When another woman saw the sailor, she thought he had purposely dressed like a woman to board the lifeboat.

No. It seems the other woman was upset that her husband hadn't been saved from the sinking ship. She complained to reporters about the sailor and other men who did board the lifeboats. Soon rumors spread about men being dressed as women.

Frank Tower — EXPOSED!

For years, people told the story of Frank Tower. Amazingly, he survived the sinking of *Titanic* and two other ships. But now this rumor has been exposed. Tower was just a myth that came out of some mistakes made in different newspapers. A man named Frank Toner did survive the sinking of another doomed ship, the *Lusitania*. A torpedo sank the liner in 1915. A crew member named William Clark survived the sinking of both *Titanic* and another ship. Somehow, the two stories were combined. They created the myth of Frank Tower and his good luck on three different doomed ships.

Did an officer kill a passenger?

What's the story?

Titanic officers carried guns. Officer William Murdoch shot one or two passengers. They tried to enter a lifeboat before they were supposed to.

THE EVIDENCE

I warn you – stand back!

BLAM!

The officers did carry guns when they were helping passengers into the lifeboats. And several times, Murdoch fired his gun into the air to keep order when people panicked. Some passengers later claimed to have seen an officer kill two people.

The VERDICT

Probably not. No one has any proof that Murdoch or any other officer shot a passenger. Most accounts say Murdoch was a hero. He helped the passengers into the lifeboats and gave up his own life jacket. He also bravely stayed on the ship while it sank. The Murdoch legend came to life again in 1997. The movie *Titanic* showed him shooting a passenger and then killing himself. Some people think another officer did kill himself before the ship sank. That possibility has kept the Murdoch mystery alive.

Officers of *Titanic*

Was there a fire on board *Titanic*?

What's the story?

A fire began on *Titanic* before the ship left Southampton, England. The fire was not put out until after *Titanic* sailed for New York.

WAIT A SECOND . . .

Like most ships of the day, *Titanic* used coal for fuel. The coal sat near the boilers that powered the engines. On any ship, the coal could catch fire. But the fire was usually put out before damaging the ship. Some people claim that coal on board *Titanic* caught fire. This fire might have weakened the steel **bulkheads**. The bulkheads were designed to contain any ocean water that entered the ship.

bulkhead — a wall that separates areas inside a ship; bulkheads help prevent fires from spreading throughout a ship.

ENGINES   COAL BUNKERS

PIER 37
SOUTHAMPTON

Yes. A coal fire did burn for several days on *Titanic*'s voyage to New York. But modern metal experts doubt that the fire weakened the bulkheads and made the ship more likely to sink. Passengers who boarded *Titanic* in England knew nothing about the fire below.

> **FACT:** Unused coal sank with *Titanic*. Divers found the coal. Some of it has been turned into jewelry.

Did the Hope diamond sink *Titanic?*

What's the story?

The Hope diamond is a large, blue diamond prized for its beauty. Some owners died horrible deaths, leading people to say the jewel was cursed. Some wealthy passengers traveled with their expensive jewels. The cursed Hope diamond was on board *Titanic*, which led to the sinking of the ship.

BUT CONSIDER THIS....

The movie *Titanic* featured a large, blue diamond called the Heart of the Ocean. That fake gem was based on the very real Hope diamond. The movie led some people to think the Hope diamond was on board *Titanic*.

The VERDICT

No. None of the *Titanic* passengers were carrying the Hope diamond. What's more, there is no curse on the Hope diamond. In 1958, the dazzling jewel was donated to the Smithsonian Institution in Washington, D.C.

Did a mummy's curse doom *Titanic*?

What's the story?

Some folks say nothing is worse than a mummy's curse. And the mummy of the Egyptian priestess Amen-Ra was in the hold of *Titanic*. The cursed mummy led to the ship's sinking.

THE EVIDENCE

In the late 1800s, four men found Princess Amen-Ra's mummy in Egypt near the Nile River. One of the men died, while another was shot in the arm. The other two men traveled back to England with the mummy. They soon suffered bad luck of their own. The mummy was eventually donated to the British Museum. In 1912, the mummy traveled on *Titanic* to reach a U.S. museum.

The VERDICT

No. There's no such thing as a mummy's curse. Also, ship records show there was no mummy on board. The British Museum never housed Princess Amen-Ra's mummy. But the museum does have a coffin lid of an unknown Egyptian priestess.

27

FACT OR FICTION?:
How to Tell the Difference

You've just read some of the most famous stories about *Titanic*. Here are three more stories about the ship. Do you think they're true or false?

1.) Shipbuilders painted the words "We defy God to sink her" on the inside of *Titanic*.

2.) The ship's band played until *Titanic* sank.

3.) Passengers in the cheapest rooms couldn't escape because crew members locked the doors in their part of the ship.

If you said all three are false, you're right. Yet there is an element of truth to the rumors. The workers didn't dare God to sink the ship. But one survivor claimed a crew member told her, "God himself could not sink this ship."

Titanic's band did play while passengers boarded the lifeboats. But by most accounts, the musicians stopped playing before the ship actually sank.

Third-class passengers were not kept from leaving the lowest parts of the ship. After *Titanic* hit the iceberg, crew members started helping people board the lifeboats. Many of the third-class passengers waited in their rooms expecting to receive additional instructions. Most of these passengers were servants or immigrants. They were used to waiting for directions. Sadly, those directions came too late for many passengers.

To sort out the truth from the rumors, you need to do good research. Learn the facts by using reliable sources. These sources include books and articles written by experts. Some Web sites may also provide accurate information. Look for Web sites connected to museums, history centers, or universities. You can also check newspapers like the *New York Times* or the *Wall Street Journal*. Ask a librarian if you're not sure whether a source is reliable or not.

Good research can help you find the truth about important events. The truth is amazing enough, so there's no need to fall for the rumors.

Glossary

bulkhead (BUHLK-hed) — a wall that separates areas inside a ship; bulkheads help prevent fires from spreading throughout a ship.

coincidence (koh-IN-si-duhnss) — a chance happening or meeting

compartment (kuhm-PART-muhnt) — a section inside a ship that is divided by walls and doors

hold (HOHLD) — the part of a ship where the cargo is stored

hull (HUHL) — the frame or body of a ship

knot (NOT) — a measurement of speed for ships; 1 knot equals 1.15 miles per hour.

luxurious (luhg-ZHOOR-ee-uhs) — marked by luxury; a luxury is something that is not needed but is enjoyable to have.

maiden voyage (MAYD-uhn VOI-ij) — a ship's first trip

theory (THEE-ur-ee) — an idea that explains something that is unknown

torpedo (tor-PEE-doh) — an underwater missile that explodes when it hits a target, such as a ship

Read More

Biskup, Agnieszka. *Exploring Titanic: An Isabel Soto History Adventure.* Graphic Expeditions. Mankato, Minn.: Capstone Press, 2010

Brown, Don. *All Stations! Distress!: April 15, 1912, The Day the Titanic Sank.* New York: Roaring Brook Press, 2008.

Peters, Stephanie True. *The First and Final Voyage: The Sinking of the Titanic.* Graphic Flash. Minneapolis: Stone Arch Books, 2008.

Internet Sites

FactHound offers a safe, fun way to find Internet sites related to this book. All of the sites on FactHound have been researched by our staff.

Here's all you do:

Visit *www.facthound.com*

FactHound will fetch the best sites for you!

Index

Amen-Ra, Princess, 27
Atlantic Ocean, 8–9

Blue Riband, 9
Britannic, 7
Brown, Molly, 19
bulkheads, 24–25

coal, 24–25

England, 7, 24, 25, 27

Gardiner, Robin, 16

Hope diamond, 26

iceberg, 12–13, 14, 29
Ireland, 8, 10

lifeboats, 18–19, 20–21, 22–23,
    28, 29
Lusitania, 21

Mauretania, 8
Murdoch, William, 22–23

New York, 7, 8, 24–25

Olympic, 7, 16–17

Robertson, Morgan, 12–13

speed records, 8–9
Stead, W. T., 13

Titanic
    building of, 10–11
    hull, 10, 11, 14–15, 17
    sinking of, 4, 6–7, 12–13,
        19, 21, 25, 26–27, 28
    speed of, 8–9
Tower, Frank, 21

Van Der Vat, Dan, 16

White Star Line, 6–7, 16
World War I, 7